MURAT

by

Alexandre Dumas

*From the set of Eight Volumes
of "Celebrated Crimes"*

Copyright © 2012 Read Books Ltd.
This book is copyright and may not be
reproduced or copied in any way without
the express permission of the publisher in writing

British Library Cataloguing-in-Publication Data
A catalogue record for this book is available from the
British Library

Contents

Alexandre Dumas 5
I—TOULON 7
II—CORSICA 22
III—PIZZO 40

Alexandre Dumas

Alexandre Dumas was born in Villers-Cotterêts, France in 1802. His parents were poor, but their heritage and good reputation – Alexandre's father had been a general in Napoleon's army – provided Alexandre with opportunities for good employment. In 1822, Dumas moved to Paris to work for future king Louis Philippe I in the Palais Royal. It was here that he began to write for magazines and the theatre.

In 1829 and 1830 respectively, Dumas produced the plays Henry III and His Court and Christine, both of which met with critical acclaim and financial success. As a result, he was able to commit himself full-time to writing. Despite the turbulent economic times which followed the Revolution of 1830, Dumas turned out to have something of an entrepreneurial streak, and did well for himself in this decade. He founded a production studio that turned out hundreds of stories under his creative direction, and began to produce serialised novels for newspapers which were widely read by the French public. It was over the next two decades, as a now famous and much loved author of romantic and adventuring sagas, that Dumas produced his best-known works – the D'Artagnan romances, including The Three Musketeers, in 1844, and The Count of Monte Cristo, in 1846.

Dumas made a lot of money from his writing, but he was almost constantly penniless as a result of his extravagant lifestyle and love of women. In 1851 he fled his creditors to Belgium, and then Russia, and then Italy, not returning to Paris until 1864. Dumas died in Puys, France, in 1870, at the age of 68. He is now enshrined in the Panthéon of Paris alongside fellow authors Victor Hugo and Emile Zola. Since his death, his fiction has been translated into almost a hundred languages, and has formed the basis for more than 200 motion pictures.

I—TOULON

On the 18th June, 1815, at the very moment when the destiny of Europe was being decided at Waterloo, a man dressed like a beggar was silently following the road from Toulon to Marseilles.

Arrived at the entrance of the Gorge of Ollioulles, he halted on a little eminence from which he could see all the surrounding country; then either because he had reached the end of his journey, or because, before attempting that forbidding, sombre pass which is called the Thermopylae of Provence, he wished to enjoy the magnificent view which spread to the southern horizon a little longer, he went and sat down on the edge of the ditch which bordered the road, turning his back on the mountains which rise like an amphitheatre to the north of the town, and having at his feet a rich plain covered with tropical vegetation, exotics of a conservatory, trees and flowers quite unknown in any other part of France.

Beyond this plain, glittering in the last rays of the sun, pale and motionless as a mirror lay the sea, and on the surface of the water glided one brig-of-war, which, taking advantage of a fresh land breeze, had all sails spread, and was bowling along rapidly, making for Italian seas. The beggar followed it eagerly with his eyes until it disappeared between the Cape of Gien and the first of the islands of Hyeres, then as the white apparition vanished he sighed deeply, let his head fall into his hands, and remained motionless and absorbed in his reflections until the tramplings of a cavalcade made him start; he looked up, shook back his long black hair, as if he wished to get rid of the gloomy thoughts which were overwhelming him, and, looking at the entrance to the gorge from whence the noise came, he soon saw two riders appear, who were no doubt well known to him, for, drawing himself up to his full height, he let fall the stick he was carrying, and folding his arms he turned towards them. On their side the new-comers had hardly seen him before they halted, and the foremost dismounted, threw his bridle to his companion, and uncovering, though fifty paces from the man in rags, advanced respectfully towards him. The beggar allowed him to approach with an air of sombre dignity and without a single movement; then, when he was quite near—

"Well, marshal, have, you news for me?" said the beggar.

"Yes, sire," said the other sadly.

"And what are they?"

"Such that I could wish it were anyone but myself to announce them to your Majesty——"

"So the Emperor refuses my services! He forgets the victories of Aboukir, Eylau, and Moscow?"

"No, sire; but he remembers the treaty of Naples, the taking of Reggio, and the declaration of war of the viceroy of Italy."

The beggar struck his forehead.

"Yes, yes! I daresay he thinks I deserve his reproaches, and yet it seems to me that he ought to remember that there are two men in me—the soldier whom he made his brother, and the brother whom he made a king.... Yes, as brother I have treated him ill—very ill, but as king, upon my soul, I could not have acted differently.... I had to choose between my sword and my crown, and between a regiment and a people. Listen, Brune: you do not know how it all happened. There was an English fleet, the guns of which were growling in the port, there was a Neapolitan population howling in the streets. If I had been alone, I would have passed through the fleet with one boat, through the crowd with my sword alone, but I had a wife and children. Yet I hesitated; the idea of being called traitor and deserter caused me to shed more tears than the loss of my throne, or perhaps the death of those I love best, will ever wring from me.... And so he will have nothing more to do with me? He refuses me as general, captain, private? Then what is left for me to do?"

"Sire, your Majesty must leave France immediately."

"And if I don't obey?"

"My orders are to arrest you and deliver you up to a court-martial!"

"Old comrade, you will not do that?"

"I shall do it, praying God to strike me dead in the moment I lay hands on you!"

"That's you all over, Brune. You have been able to remain a good, loyal fellow. He did not give you a kingdom, he did not encircle your brow with a band of iron which men call a crown and which drives one mad; he did not place you between your conscience and your family. So I must leave France, begin my vagabond life again, and say farewell to

Toulon, which recalls so many memories to me! See, Brune," continued Murat, leaning on the arm of the marshal, "are not the pines yonder as fine as any at the Villa Pamfili, the palms as imposing as any at Cairo, the mountains as grand as any range in the Tyrol? Look to your left, is not Cape Gien something like Castellamare and Sorrento—leaving out Vesuvius? And see, Saint-Mandrier at the farthest point of the gulf, is it not like my rock of Capri, which Lamarque juggled away so cleverly from that idiot of a Sir Hudson Lowe? My God! and I must leave all this! Is there no way of remaining on this little corner of French ground—tell me, Brune!"

"You'll break my heart, sire!" answered the marshal.

"Well, we'll say no more about it. What news?"

"The Emperor has left Paris to join the army. They must be fighting now."

"Fighting now and I not there! Oh, I feel I could have been of use to him on this battlefield. How I would have gloried in charging those miserable Prussians and dastardly English! Brune, give me a passport, I'll go at full speed, I'll reach the army, I will make myself known to some colonel, I shall say, 'Give me your regiment.' I'll charge at its head, and if the Emperor does not clasp my hand to-night, I'll blow my brains out, I swear I will. Do what I ask, Brune, and however it may end, my eternal gratitude will be yours!"

"I cannot, sire."

"Well, well, say no more about it."

"And your Majesty is going to leave France?"

"I don't know. Obey your orders, marshal, and if you come across me again, have me arrested. That's another way of doing something for me. Life is a heavy burden nowadays. He who will relieve me of it will be welcome.... Good-bye, Brune."

He held out his hand to the marshal, who tried to kiss it; but Murat opened his arms, the two old comrades held each other fast for a moment, with swelling hearts and eyes full of tears; then at last they parted. Brune remounted his horse, Murat picked up his stick again, and the two men went away in opposite directions, one to meet his death by assassination at Avignon, the other to be shot at Pizzo. Meanwhile, like Richard III, Napoleon was bartering his crown against a horse at Waterloo.

After the interview that has just been related, Murat took refuge with his nephew, who was called Bonafoux, and who was captain of a frigate; but this retreat could only be temporary, for the relationship would inevitably awake the suspicions of the authorities. In consequence, Bonafoux set about finding a more secret place of refuge for his uncle. He hit on one of his friends, an avocat, a man famed for his integrity, and that very evening Bonafoux went to see him.

After chatting on general subjects, he asked his friend if he had not a house at the seaside, and receiving an affirmative answer, he invited himself to breakfast there the next day; the proposal naturally enough was agreed to with pleasure. The next day at the appointed hour Bonafoux arrived at Bonette, which was the name of the country house where

M. Marouin's wife and daughter were staying. M. Marouin himself was kept by his work at Toulon. After the ordinary greetings, Bonafoux stepped to the window, beckoning to Marouin to rejoin him.

"I thought," he said uneasily, "that your house was by the sea."

"We are hardly ten minutes' walk from it."

"But it is not in sight."

"That hill prevents you from seeing it."

"May we go for a stroll on the beach before breakfast is served?"

"By all means. Well, your horse is still saddled. I will order mine—I will come back for you."

Marouin went out. Bonafoux remained at the window, absorbed in his thoughts. The ladies of the house, occupied in preparations for the meal, did not observe, or did not appear to observe, his preoccupation. In five minutes Marouin came back. He was ready to start. The avocat and his friend mounted their horses and rode quickly down to the sea. On the beach the captain slackened his pace, and riding along the shore for about half an hour, he seemed to be examining the bearings of the coast with great attention. Marouin followed without inquiring into his investigations, which seemed natural enough for a naval officer.

After about an hour the two men went back to the house.

Marouin wished to have the horses unsaddled, but Bonafoux objected, saying that he must go back to Toulon immediately after lunch. Indeed, the coffee was hardly finished before he rose and took leave of his hosts. Marouin, called back to town by his work, mounted his horse too, and the two friends rode back to Toulon together. After riding along for ten minutes, Bonafoux went close to his companion and touched him on the thigh—

"Marouin," he said, "I have an important secret to confide to you."

"Speak, captain. After a father confessor, you know there is no one so discreet as a notary, and after a notary an avocat."

"You can quite understand that I did not come to your country house just for the pleasure of the ride. A more important object, a serious responsibility, preoccupied me; I have chosen you out of all my friends, believing that you were devoted enough to me to render me a great service."

"You did well, captain."

"Let us go straight to the point, as men who respect and trust each other should do. My uncle, King Joachim, is proscribed, he has taken refuge with me; but he cannot remain there, for I am the first person they will suspect. Your house is in an isolated position, and consequently we could not find a better retreat for him. You must put it at our disposal until events enable the king to come to some decision."

"It is at your service," said Marouin.

"Right. My uncle shall sleep there to-night."

"But at least give me time to make some preparations worthy of my royal guest."

"My poor Marouin, you are giving yourself unnecessary trouble, and making a vexatious delay for us: King Joachim is no longer accustomed to palaces and courtiers; he is only too happy nowadays to find a cottage with a friend in it; besides, I have let him know about it, so sure was I of your answer. He is counting on sleeping at your house to-night, and if I try to change his determination now he will see a refusal in what is only a postponement, and you will lose all the credit for your generous and noble action. There—it is agreed: to-night at ten at the Champs de Mars."

With these words the captain put his horse to a gallop and disappeared. Marouin turned his horse and went back to his country house to give the necessary orders for the reception of a stranger whose name he did not mention.

At ten o'clock at night, as had been agreed, Marouin was on the Champs de Mars, then covered with Marshal Brune's field-artillery. No one had arrived yet. He walked up and down between the gun-carriages until a functionary came to ask what he was doing. He was hard put to it to find an answer: a man is hardly likely to be wandering about in an artillery park at ten o'clock at night for the mere pleasure of the thing. He asked to see the commanding officer. The officer came up: M. Marouin informed him that he was an avocat, attached to the law courts of Toulon, and told him that he had arranged to meet someone on the Champs de Mars, not knowing that it was prohibited, and that he was still waiting for that person. After this explanation, the officer authorised him to remain, and went back to his quarters. The sentinel, a faithful adherent to discipline, continued to pace up and down with his measured step, without troubling any more about the stranger's presence.

A few moments later a group of several persons appeared from the direction of Les Lices. The night was magnificent, and the moon brilliant. Marouin recognised Bonafoux, and went up to him. The captain at once took him by the hand and led him to the king, and speaking in turn to each of them—

"Sire," he said, "here is the friend. I told you of."

Then turning to Marouin—

"Here," he said, "is the King of Naples, exile and fugitive, whom I confide to your care. I do not speak of the possibility that some day he may get back his crown, that would deprive you of the credit of your fine action.... Now, be his guide—we will follow at a distance. March!"

The king and the lawyer set out at once together. Murat was dressed in a blue coat-semi-military, semi-civil, buttoned to the throat; he wore white trousers and top boots with spurs; he had long hair, moustache, and thick whiskers, which would reach round his neck.

As they rode along he questioned his host about the situation of his country house and the facility for reaching the sea in case of a surprise. Towards midnight the king and Marouin arrived at Bonette; the royal suite came up in about ten minutes; it consisted of about thirty individuals. After partaking of some light refreshment, this little troop, the last of the court of the deposed king, retired to disperse in the town and its environs, and Murat remained alone with the women, only keeping one valet named Leblanc.

Murat stayed nearly a month in this retirement, spending all his time in answering the newspapers which accused him of treason to the Emperor. This accusation was his absorbing idea, a phantom, a spectre to him; day and night he tried to shake it off, seeking in the difficult position in which he had found himself all the reasons which it might offer him for acting as he had acted. Meanwhile the terrible news of the defeat at Waterloo had spread abroad. The Emperor who had exiled him was an exile himself, and he was waiting at Rochefort, like Murat at Toulon, to hear what his enemies would decide against him. No one knows to this day what inward prompting Napoleon obeyed when, rejecting the counsels of General Lallemande and the devotion of Captain Bodin, he preferred England to America, and went like a modern Prometheus to be chained to the rock of St. Helena.

We are going to relate the fortuitous circumstance which led Murat to the moat of Pizzo, then we will leave it to fatalists to draw from this strange story whatever philosophical deduction may please them. We, as humble annalists, can only vouch for the truth of the facts we have already related and of those which will follow.

King Louis XVIII remounted his throne, consequently Murat lost all hope of remaining in France; he felt he was bound to go. His nephew Bonafoux fitted out a frigate for the United States under the name of Prince Rocca Romana. The whole suite went on board, and they began to carry on to the boat all the valuables which the exile had been able to save from the shipwreck of his kingdom. First a bag of gold weighing nearly a hundred pounds, a sword-sheath on which were the portraits of the king, the queen, and their children, the deed of the civil estates of his family bound in velvet and adorned with his arms. Murat carried on his person a belt where some precious papers were concealed, with about a score of unmounted diamonds, which he estimated himself to be worth four millions.

When all these preparations for departing were accomplished, it was agreed that the next day, the 1st of August, at five o'clock, a boat should fetch the king to the brig from a little bay, ten minutes' walk from the house where he was staying. The king spent the night making out a route for M. Marouin by which he could reach the queen, who was then in Austria, I think.

It was finished just as it was time to leave, and on crossing the threshold of the hospitable house where he had found refuge he gave it to his host, slipped into a volume of a pocket edition of Voltaire. Below the story of 'Micromegas' the king had written: [The volume is still in the hands of M. Marouin, at Toulon.]

Reassure yourself, dear Caroline; although unhappy, I am free. I am departing, but I do not know whither I am bound. Wherever I may be my heart will be with you and my children. "J. M."

Ten minutes later Murat and his host were waiting on the beach at Bonette for the boat which was to take them out to the ship.

They waited until midday, and nothing appeared; and yet

on the horizon they could see the brig which was to be his refuge, unable to lie at anchor on account of the depth of water, sailing along the coast at the risk of giving the alarm to the sentinels.

At midday the king, worn out with fatigue and the heat of the sun, was lying on the beach, when a servant arrived, bringing various refreshments, which Madame Marouin, being very uneasy, had sent at all hazards to her husband. The king took a glass of wine and water and ate an orange, and got up for a moment to see whether the boat he was expecting was nowhere visible on the vastness of the sea. There was not a boat in sight, only the brig tossing gracefully on the horizon, impatient to be off, like a horse awaiting its master.

The king sighed and lay down again on the sand.

The servant went back to Bonette with a message summoning M. Marouin's brother to the beach. He arrived in a few minutes, and almost immediately afterwards galloped off at full speed to Toulon, in order to find out from M. Bonafoux why the boat had not been sent to the king. On reaching the captain's house, he found it occupied by an armed force. They were making a search for Murat.

The messenger at last made his way through the tumult to the person he was in search of, and he heard that the boat had started at the appointed time, and that it must have gone astray in the creeks of Saint Louis and Sainte Marguerite. This was, in fact, exactly what had happened.

By five o'clock M. Marouin had reported the news to

his brother and the king. It was bad news. The king had no courage left to defend his life even by flight, he was in a state of prostration which sometimes overwhelms the strongest of men, incapable of making any plan for his own safety, and leaving M. Marouin to do the best he could. Just then a fisherman was coming into harbour singing. Marouin beckoned to him, and he came up.

Marouin began by buying all the man's fish; then, when he had paid him with a few coins, he let some gold glitter before his eyes, and offered him three louis if he would take a passenger to the brig which was lying off the Croix-des-Signaux. The fisherman agreed to do it. This chance of escape gave back Murat all his strength; he got up, embraced Marouin, and begged him to go to the queen with the volume of Voltaire. Then he sprang into the boat, which instantly left the shore.

It was already some distance from the land when the king stopped the man who was rowing and signed to Marouin that he had forgotten something. On the beach lay a bag into which Murat had put a magnificent pair of pistols mounted with silver gilt which the queen had given him, and which he set great store on. As soon as he was within hearing he shouted his reason for returning to his host. Marouin seized the valise, and without waiting for Murat to land he threw it into the boat; the bag flew open, and one of the pistols fell out. The fisherman only glanced once at the royal weapon, but it was enough to make him notice its richness and to arouse his suspicions. Nevertheless, he went on rowing towards the frigate. M. Marouin seeing him disappear in the distance, left his brother on the beach, and bowing once more to the king, returned to the house to calm his wife's anxieties and to take the repose of which he was in much need.

Two hours later he was awakened. His house was to be searched in its turn by soldiers. They searched every nook and corner without finding a trace of the king. Just as they were getting desperate, the brother came in; Maroum smiled at him; believing the king to be safe, but by the new-comer's expression he saw that some fresh misfortune was in the wind. In the first moment's respite given him by his visitors he went up to his brother.

"Well," he said, "I hope the king is on board?"

"The king is fifty yards away, hidden in the outhouse."

"Why did he come back?"

"The fisherman pretended he was afraid of a sudden squall, and refused to take him off to the brig."

"The scoundrel!"

The soldiers came in again.

They spent the night in fruitless searching about the house and buildings; several times they passed within a few steps of the king, and he could hear their threats and imprecations. At last, half an hour before dawn, they went away. Marouin watched them go, and when they were out of sight he ran to the king. He found him lying in a corner, a pistol clutched in each hand. The unhappy man had been overcome by fatigue and had fallen asleep. Marouin hesitated a moment to bring him back to his wandering, tormented life, but there was not a minute to lose. He woke him.

They went down to the beach at once. A morning mist lay over the sea. They could not see anything two hundred yards ahead. They were obliged to wait. At last the first sunbeams began to pierce this nocturnal mist. It slowly dispersed, gliding over the sea as clouds move in the sky. The king's hungry eye roved over the tossing waters before him, but he saw nothing, yet he could not banish the hope that somewhere behind that moving curtain he would find his refuge. Little by little the horizon came into view; light wreaths of mist, like smoke, still floated about the surface of the water, and in each of them the king thought he recognised the white sails of his vessel. The last gradually vanished, the sea was revealed in all its immensity, it was deserted. Not daring to delay any longer, the ship had sailed away in the night.

"So," said the king, "the die is cast. I will go to Corsica."

The same day Marshal Brune was assassinated at Avignon.

II—CORSICA

Once more on the same beach at Bonette, in the same bay where he had awaited the boat in vain, still attended by his band of faithful followers, we find Murat on the 22nd August in the same year. It was no longer by Napoleon that he was threatened, it was by Louis XVIII that he was proscribed; it was no longer the military loyalty of Marshal Brune who came with tears in his eyes to give notice of the orders he had received, but the ungrateful hatred of M. de Riviere, who had set a price [48,000 francs.] on the head of the man who had saved his own.[Conspiracy of Pichegru.] M. de Riviere had indeed written to the ex-King of Naples advising him to abandon himself to the good faith and humanity of the King of France, but his vague invitation had not seemed sufficient guarantee to the outlaw, especially on the part of one who had allowed the assassination almost before his eyes of a man who carried a safe-conduct signed by himself. Murat knew of the massacre of the Mamelukes at Marseilles, the assassination of Brune at Avignon; he had been warned the day before by the police of Toulon that a formal order for his arrest was out; thus it was impossible that he should remain any longer in France. Corsica, with its hospitable towns, its friendly mountains, its impenetrable forests, was hardly fifty leagues distant; he must reach Corsica, and wait in its towns, mountains, and forests until the crowned heads of Europe should decide the fate of the man they had called brother for seven years.

At ten o'clock at, night the king went down to the shore. The boat which was to take him across had not reached the rendezvous, but this time there was not the slightest fear that it would fail; the bay had been reconnoitred during the day by three men devoted to the fallen fortunes of the king—Messieurs Blancard, Langlade, and Donadieu, all three naval officers, men of ability and warm heart, who had sworn by their own lives to convey Murat to Corsica, and who were in fact risking their lives in order to accomplish their promise. Murat saw the deserted shore without uneasiness, indeed this delay afforded him a few more moments of patriotic satisfaction.

On this little patch of land, this strip of sand, the unhappy exile clung to his mother France, for once his foot touched the vessel which was to carry him away, his separation from France would be long, if not eternal. He started suddenly amidst these thoughts and sighed: he had just perceived a sail gliding over the waves like a phantom through the transparent darkness of the southern night. Then a sailor's song was heard; Murat recognised the appointed signal, and answered it by burning the priming of a pistol, and the boat immediately ran inshore; but as she drew three feet of water, she was obliged to stop ten or twelve feet from the beach; two men dashed into the water and reached the beach, while a third remained crouching in the stern-sheets wrapped in his boat-cloak.

"Well, my good friends," said the king, going towards Blancard and Langlade until he felt the waves wet his feet "the moment is come, is it not? The wind is favourable, the sea calm, we must get to sea."

"Yes," answered Langlade, "yes, we must start; and yet perhaps it would be wiser to wait till to-morrow."

"Why?" asked Murat.

Langlade did not answer, but turning towards the west, he raised his hand, and according to the habit of sailors, he whistled to call the wind.

"That's no good," said Donadieu, who had remained in the boat. "Here are the first gusts; you will have more than you know what to do with in a minute.... Take care, Langlade, take care! Sometimes in calling the wind you wake up a storm."

Murat started, for he thought that this warning which rose from the sea had been given him by the spirit of the waters; but the impression was a passing one, and he recovered himself in a moment.

"All the better," he said; "the more wind we have, the faster we shall go."

"Yes," answered Langlade, "but God knows where it will take us if it goes on shifting like this."

"Don't start to-night, sire," said Blancard, adding his voice to those of his two companions.

"But why not?"

"You see that bank of black cloud there, don't you? Well, at sunset it was hardly visible, now it covers a good part of the sky, in an hour there won't be a star to be seen."

"Are you afraid?" asked Murat.

"Afraid!" answered Langlade. "Of what? Of the storm? I might as well ask if your Majesty is afraid of a cannon-ball. We have demurred solely on your account, sire; do you think seadogs like ourselves would delay on account of the storm?"

"Then let us go!" cried Murat, with a sigh.

"Good-bye, Marouin.... God alone can reward you for what you have done for me. I am at your orders, gentlemen."

At these words the two sailors seized the king end hoisted him on to their shoulders, and carried him into the sea; in another moment he was on board. Langlade and Blancard sprang in behind him. Donadieu remained at the helm, the two other officers undertook the management of the boat, and began their work by unfurling the sails. Immediately the pinnace seemed to rouse herself like a horse at touch of the spur; the sailors cast a careless glance back, and Murat feeling that they were sailing away, turned towards his host and called for a last time—

"You have your route as far as Trieste. Do not forget my wife!... Good-bye-good-bye——!"

"God keep you, sire!" murmured Marouin.

And for some time, thanks to the white sail which gleamed through the darkness, he could follow with his eyes the boat which was rapidly disappearing; at last it vanished altogether. Marouin lingered on the shore, though he could see nothing; then he heard a cry, made faint by the distance; it was Murat's last adieu to France.

When M. Marouin was telling me these details one evening on the very spot where it all happened, though twenty years had passed, he remembered clearly the slightest incidents of the embarkation that night. From that moment he assured me that a presentiment of misfortune seized him; he could not tear himself away from the shore, and several times he longed to call the king back, but, like a man in a dream, he opened his mouth without being able to utter a sound. He was afraid of being thought foolish, and it was not until one o'clock that is, two and a half hours after the departure of the boat-that he went home with a sad and heavy heart.

The adventurous navigators had taken the course from Toulon to Bastia, and at first it seemed to the king that the sailors' predictions were belied; the wind, instead of getting up, fell little by little, and two hours after the departure the boat was rocking without moving forward or backward on the waves, which were sinking from moment to moment. Murat sadly watched the phosphorescent furrow trailing behind the little boat: he had nerved himself to face a storm, but not a dead calm, and without even interrogating his companions, of whose uneasiness he took no account, he lay down in the boat, wrapped in his cloak, closing his eyes as if he were asleep, and following the flow of his thoughts, which were far more tumultuous than that of the waters. Soon the two sailors, thinking him asleep, joined the pilot, and sitting down beside the helm, they began to consult together.

"You were wrong, Langlade," said Donadieu, "in choosing a craft like this, which is either too small or else too big; in an open boat we can never weather a storm, and without oars we can never make any way in a calm."

"'Fore God! I had no choice. I was obliged to take what I could get, and if it had not been the season for tunny-fishing I might not even have got this wretched pinnace, or rather I should have had to go into the harbour to find it, and they keep such a sharp lookout that I might well have gone in without coming out again."

"At least it is seaworthy," said Blancard.

"Pardieu, you know what nails and planks are when they have been soaked in sea-water for ten years. On any ordinary occasion, a man would rather not go in her from Marseilles to the Chateau d'If, but on an occasion like this one would willingly go round the world in a nutshell."

"Hush!" said Donadieu. The sailors listened; a distant growl was heard, but it was so faint that only the experienced ear of a sailor could have distinguished it.

"Yes, yes," said Langlade, "it is a warning for those who have legs or wings to regain the homes and nests that they ought never to have left."

"Are we far from the islands?" asked Donadieu quickly.

"About a mile off."

"Steer for them."

"What for?" asked Murat, looking up.

"To put in there, sire, if we can."

"No, no," cried Murat; "I will not land except in Corsica. I will not leave France again. Besides, the sea is calm and the wind is getting up again—"

"Down with the sails!" shouted Donadieu. Instantly

Langlade and Blancard jumped forward to carry out the order. The sail slid down the mast and fell in a heap in the bottom of the boat.

"What are you doing?" cried Murat. "Do you forget that I am king and that I command you?"

"Sire," said Donadieu, "there is a king more powerful than you—God; there is a voice which drowns yours—the voice of the tempest: let us save your Majesty if possible, and demand nothing more of us."

Just then a flash of lightning quivered along the horizon, a clap of thunder nearer than the first one was heard, a light foam appeared on the surface of the water, and the boat trembled like a living thing. Murat began to understand that danger was approaching, then he got up smiling, threw his hat behind him, shook back his long hair, and breathed in the storm like the smell of powder—the soldier was ready for the battle.

"Sire," said Donadieu, "you have seen many a battle, but perhaps you have never watched a storm if you are curious about it, cling to the mast, for you have a fine opportunity now."

"What ought I to do?" said Murat. "Can I not help you in any way?"

"No, not just now, sire; later you will be useful at the pumps."

During this dialogue the storm had drawn near; it rushed on the travellers like a war-horse, breathing out fire and wind through its nostrils, neighing like thunder, and scattering the foam of the waves beneath its feet.

Donadieu turned the rudder, the boat yielded as if it understood the necessity for prompt obedience, and presented the poop to the shock of wind; then the squall passed, leaving the sea quivering, and everything was calm again. The storm took breath.

"Will that gust be all?" asked Murat.

"No, your Majesty, that was the advance-guard only; the body of the army will be up directly."

"And are you not going to prepare for it?" asked the king gaily.

"What could we do?" said Donadieu. "We have not an inch of canvas to catch the wind, and as long as we do not make too much water, we shall float like a cork. Look out-sire!"

Indeed, a second hurricane was on its way, bringing rain and lightning; it was swifter than the first. Donadieu endeavoured to repeat the same manoeuvre, but he could not turn before the wind struck the boat, the mast bent like a reed; the boat shipped a wave.

"To the pumps!" cried Donadieu. "Sire, now is the moment to help us—"

Blancard, Langlade, and Murat seized their hats and began to bale out the boat. The position of the four men was terrible—it lasted three hours.

At dawn the wind fell, but the sea was still high. They began to feel the need of food: all the provisions had been spoiled by sea-water, only the wine had been preserved from its contact.

The king took a bottle and swallowed a little wine first, then he passed it to his companions, who drank in their turn: necessity had overcome etiquette. By chance Langlade had on him a few chocolates, which he offered to the king. Murat divided them into four equal parts, and forced his companions to take their shares; then, when the meal was over, they steered for Corsica, but the boat had suffered so much that it was improbable that it would reach Bastia.

The whole day passed without making ten miles; the boat was kept under the jib, as they dared not hoist the mainsail, and the wind was so variable that much time was lost in humouring its caprices.

By evening the boat had drawn a considerable amount of water, it penetrated between the boards, the handkerchiefs of the crew served to plug up the leaks, and night, which was descending in mournful gloom, wrapped them a second time in darkness. Prostrated with fatigue, Murat fell asleep, Blancard and Langlade took their places beside Donadieu, and the three men, who seemed insensible to the calls of sleep and fatigue, watched over his slumbers.

The night was calm enough apparently, but low grumblings were heard now and then.

The three sailors looked at each other strangely and then at the king, who was sleeping at the bottom of the boat, his cloak soaked with sea-water, sleeping as soundly as he had slept on the sands of Egypt or the snows of Russia.

Then one of them got up and went to the other end of

the boat, whistling between his teeth a Provencal air; then, after examining the sky, the waves; and the boat, he went back to his comrades and sat down, muttering, "Impossible! Except by a miracle, we shall never make the land."

The night passed through all its phases. At dawn there was a vessel in sight.

"A sail!" cried Donadieu,—"a sail!"

At this cry the king—awoke; and soon a little trading brig hove in sight, going from Corsica to Toulon.

Donadieu steered for the brig, Blancard hoisted enough sail to work the boat, and Langlade ran to the prow and held up the king's cloak on the end of a sort of harpoon. Soon the voyagers perceived that they had been sighted, the brig went about to approach them, and in ten minutes they found themselves within fifty yards of it. The captain appeared in the bows. Then the king hailed him and offered him a substantial reward if he would receive them on board and take them to Corsica. The captain listened to the proposal; then immediately turning to the crew, he gave an order in an undertone which Donadieu could not hear, but which he understood probably by the gesture, for he instantly gave Langlade and Blancard the order to make away from the schooner. They obeyed with the unquestioning promptitude of sailors; but the king stamped his foot.

"What are you doing, Donadieu? What are you about? Don't you see that she is coming up to us?"

"Yes—upon my soul—so she is.... Do as I say, Langlade; ready, Blancard. Yes, she is coming upon us, and perhaps I was too late in seeing this. That's all right—that's all right: my part now."

Then he forced over the rudder, giving it so violent a jerk that the boat, forced to change her course suddenly, seemed to rear and plunge like a horse struggling against the curb; finally she obeyed. A huge wave, raised by the giant bearing down on the pinnace, carried it on like a leaf, and the brig passed within a few feet of the stern.

"Ah!.... traitor!" cried the king, who had only just begun to realise the intention of the captain. At the same time, he pulled a pistol from his belt, crying "Board her! board her!" and tried to fire on the brig, but the powder was wet and would not catch. The king was furious, and went on shouting "Board her! board her!"

"Yes, the wretch, or rather the imbecile," said Donadieu, "he took us for pirates, and wanted to sink us—as if we needed him to do that!"

Indeed, a single glance at the boat showed that she was beginning to make water.

The effort—to escape which Donadieu had made had strained the boat terribly, and the water was pouring in by a number of leaks between the planks; they had to begin again bailing out with their hats, and went on at it for ten hours. Then for the second time Donadieu heard the consoling cry, "A sail! a sail!" The king and his companions immediately left off bailing; they hoisted the sails again, and steered for the vessel which was coming towards them, and neglected to fight against the water, which was rising rapidly.

From that time forth it was a question of time, of minutes, of seconds; it was a question of reaching the ship before the boat foundered.

The vessel, however, seemed to understand the desperate position of the men imploring help; she was coming up at full speed. Langlade was the first to recognise her; she was a Government felucca plying between Toulon and Bastia. Langlade was a friend of the captain, and he called his name with the penetrating voice of desperation, and he was heard. It was high time: the water kept on rising, and the king and his companions were already up to their knees; the boat groaned in its death-struggle; it stood still, and began to go round and round.

Just then two or three ropes thrown from the felucca fell upon the boat; the king seized one, sprang forward, and reached the rope-ladder: he was saved.

Blancard and Langlade immediately followed. Donadieu waited until the last, as was his duty, and as he put his foot on the ladder he felt the other boat begin to go under; he turned round with all a sailor's calm, and saw the gulf open its jaws beneath him, and then the shattered boat capsized, and immediately disappeared. Five seconds more, and the four men who were saved would have been lost beyond recall! [These details are well known to the people of Toulon, and I have heard them myself a score of times during the two stays that I made in that town during 1834 and 1835. Some of the people who related them had them first-hand from Langlade and Donadieu themselves.]

Murat had hardly gained the deck before a man came and fell at his feet: it was a Mameluke whom he had taken to Egypt in former years, and had since married at Castellamare; business affairs had taken him to Marseilles, where by a miracle he had escaped the massacre of his comrades, and in spite of his disguise and fatigue he had recognised his former master.

His exclamations of joy prevented the king from keeping up his incognito. Then Senator Casabianca, Captain Oletta, a nephew of Prince Baciocchi, a staff-paymaster called Boerco, who were themselves fleeing from the massacres of the South, were all on board the vessel, and improvising a little court, they greeted the king with the title of "your Majesty." It had been a sudden embarkation, it brought about a swift change: he was no longer Murat the exile; he was Joachim, the King of Naples. The exile's refuge disappeared with the foundered boat; in its place Naples and its magnificent gulf appeared on the horizon like a marvellous mirage, and no doubt the primary idea of the fatal expedition of Calabria was originated in the first days of exultation which followed those hours of anguish. The king, however, still uncertain of the welcome which awaited him in Corsica, took the name of the Count of Campo Melle, and it was under this name that he landed at Bastia on the 25th August. But this precaution was useless; three days after his arrival, not a soul but knew of his presence in the town.

Crowds gathered at once, and cries of "Long live Joachim!" were heard, and the king, fearing to disturb the public peace, left Bastia the same evening with his three companions and his Mameluke. Two hours later he arrived at Viscovato, and knocked at the door of General Franceschetti, who had been in his service during his whole reign, and who, leaving Naples at the same time as the king, had gone to Corsica with his wife, to live with his father-in-law, M. Colonna Cicaldi.

He was in the middle of supper when a servant told him that a stranger was asking to speak to him—he went out, and found Murat wrapped in a military greatcoat, a sailor's cap drawn down on his head, his beard grown long, and wearing a soldier's trousers, boots, and gaiters.

The general stood still in amazement; Murat fixed his great dark eyes on him, and then, folding his arms:—

"Franceschetti," said he, "have you room at your table for your general, who is hungry? Have you a shelter under your roof for your king, who is an exile?"

Franceschetti looked astonished as he recognised Joachim, and could only answer him by falling on his knees and kissing his hand. From that moment the general's house was at Murat's disposal.

The news of the king's arrival had hardly been handed about the neighbourhood before officers of all ranks hastened to Viscovato, veterans who had fought under him, Corsican hunters who were attracted by his adventurous character; in a few days the general's house was turned into a palace, the village into a royal capital, the island into a kingdom.

Strange rumours were heard concerning Murat's intentions. An army of nine hundred men helped to give them some amount of confirmation. It was then that Blancard, Donadieu, and Langlade took leave of him; Murat wished to keep them, but they had been vowed to the rescue of the exile, not to the fortunes of the king.

We have related how Murat had met one of his former Mamelukes, a man called Othello, on board the Bastia mailboat. Othello had followed him to Viscovato, and the ex-King of Naples considered how to make use of him. Family relations recalled him naturally to Castellamare, and Murat ordered him to return there, entrusting to him letters for persons on whose devotion he could depend. Othello started, and reached his father-in-law's safely, and thought he could confide in him; but the latter was horror-struck, and alarmed the police, who made a descent on Othello one night, and seized the letters.

The next day each man to whom a letter was addressed was arrested and ordered to answer Murat as if all was well, and to point out Salerno as the best place for disembarking: five out of seven were dastards enough to obey; the two remaining, who were two Spanish brothers, absolutely refused; they were thrown into a dungeon.

However, on the 17th September, Murat left Viscovato; General Franceschetti and several Corsican officers served as escort; he took the road to Ajaccio by Cotone, the mountains of Serra and Bosco, Venaco and Vivaro, by the gorges of the forest of Vezzanovo and Bogognone; he was received and feted like a king everywhere, and at the gates of the towns he was met by deputations who made him speeches and saluted him with the title of "Majesty"; at last, on the 23rd September, he arrived at Ajaccio. The whole population awaited him outside the walls, and his entry into the town was a triumphal procession; he was taken to the inn which had been fixed upon beforehand by the quartermasters. It was enough to turn the head of a man less impressionable than Murat; as for him, he was intoxicated with it. As he went into the inn he held out his hand to Franceschetti.

"You see," he said, "what the Neapolitans will do for me by the way the Corsicans receive me."

It was the first mention which had escaped him of his plans for the future, and from that very day he began to give orders for his departure.

They collected ten little feluccas: a Maltese, named Barbara, former captain of a frigate of the Neapolitan navy, was appointed commander-in-chief of the expedition; two hundred and fifty men were recruited and ordered to hold themselves in readiness for the first signal.

Murat was only waiting for the answers to Othello's letters: they arrived on the afternoon of the 28th. Murat invited all his officers to a grand dinner, and ordered double pay and double rations to the men.

The king was at dessert when the arrival of M. Maceroni was announced to him: he was the envoy of the foreign powers who brought Murat the answer which he had been awaiting so long at Toulon. Murat left the table and went into another room. M. Maceroni introduced himself as charged with an official mission, and handed the king the Emperor of

Austria's ultimatum. It was couched in the following terms:

"Monsieur Maceroni is authorised by these presents to announce to King Joachim that His Majesty the Emperor of Austria will afford him shelter in his States on the following terms:—

"1. The king is to take a private name. The queen having adopted that of Lipano, it is proposed that the king should do likewise.

"2. It will be permitted to the king to choose a town in Bohemia, Moravia, or the Tyrol, as a place of residence. He could even inhabit a country house in one of these same provinces without inconvenience.

"3. The king is to give his word of honour to His Imperial and Royal Majesty that he will never leave the States of Austria without the express-permission of the Emperor, and that he is to live like a private gentleman of distinction, but submitting to the laws in force in the States of Austria.

"In attestation whereof, and to guard against abuse, the undersigned has received the order of the Emperor to sign the present declaration.

"(Signed) PRINCE OF METTERNICH
"PARIS, 1st Sept. 1815."

Murat smiled as he finished reading, then he signed to

M. Maceroni to follow him:

He led him on to the terrace of the house, which looked over the whole town, and over which a banner floated as it might on a royal castle. From thence they could see Ajaccio all gay and illuminated, the port with its little fleet, and the streets crowded with people, as if it were a fete-day.

Hardly had the crowd set eyes on Murat before a universal cry arose, "Long live Joachim, brother of Napoleon! Long live the King of Naples!"

Murat bowed, and the shouts were redoubled, and the garrison band played the national airs.

M. Maceroni did not know how to believe his own eyes and ears.

When the king had enjoyed his astonishment, he invited him to go down to the drawing-room. His staff were there, all in full uniform: one might have been at Caserte or at Capo di Monte. At last, after a moment's hesitation, Maceroni approached Murat.

"Sir," he said, "what is my answer to be to His Majesty the Emperor of Austria?"

"Sir," answered Murat, with the lofty dignity which sat so well on his fine face, "tell my brother Francis what you have seen and heard, and add that I am setting out this very night to reconquer my kingdom of Naples."

III—PIZZO

The letters which had made Murat resolve to leave Corsica had been brought to him by a Calabrian named Luidgi. He had presented himself to the king as the envoy of the Arab, Othello, who had been thrown into prison in Naples, as we have related, as well as the seven recipients of the letters.

The answers, written by the head of the Neapolitan police, indicated the port of Salerno as the best place for Joachim to land; for King Ferdinand had assembled three thousand Austrian troops at that point, not daring to trust the Neapolitan soldiers, who cherished a brilliant and enthusiastic memory of Murat.

Accordingly the flotilla was directed for the Gulf of Salerno, but within sight of the island of Capri a violent storm broke over it, and drove it as far as Paola, a little seaport situated ten miles from Cosenza. Consequently the vessels were anchored for the night of the 5th of October in a little indentation of the coast not worthy of the name of a roadstead. The king, to remove all suspicion from the coastguards and the Sicilian scorridori, [Small vessels fitted up as ships-of-war.] ordered that all lights should be extinguished and that the vessels should tack about during the night; but towards one o'clock such a violent land-wind sprang up that the expedition was driven out to sea, so that on the 6th at dawn the king's vessel was alone.

During the morning they overhauled Captain Cicconi's

felucca, and the two ships dropped anchor at four o'clock in sight of Santo-Lucido. In the evening the king commanded Ottoviani, a staff officer, to go ashore and reconnoitre. Luidgi offered to accompany him. Murat accepted his services. So Ottoviani and his guide went ashore, whilst Cicconi and his felucca put out to sea in search of the rest of the fleet.

Towards eleven o'clock at night the lieutenant of the watch descried a man in the waves swimming to the vessel. As soon as he was within hearing the lieutenant hailed him. The swimmer immediately made himself known: it was Luidgi. They put out the boat, and he came on board. Then he told them that Ottoviani had been arrested, and he had only escaped himself by jumping into the sea. Murat's first idea was to go to the rescue of Ottoviani; but Luidgi made the king realise the danger and uselessness of such an attempt; nevertheless, Joachim remained agitated and irresolute until two o'clock in the morning.

At last he gave the order to put to sea again. During the manoeuvre which effected this a sailor fell overboard and disappeared before they had time to help him. Decidedly these were ill omens.

On the morning of the 7th two vessels were in sight. The king gave the order to prepare for action, but Barbara recognised them as Cicconi's felucca and Courrand's lugger, which had joined each other and were keeping each other company. They hoisted the necessary signals, and the two captains brought up their vessels alongside the admiral's.

While they were deliberating as to what route to follow, a

boat came up to Murat's vessel. Captain Pernice was on board with a lieutenant. They came to ask the king's permission to board his ship, not wishing to remain on Courrand's, for in their opinion he was a traitor.

Murat sent to fetch him, and in spite of his protestations he was made to descend into a boat with fifty men, and the boat was moored to the vessel. The order was carried out at once, and the little squadron advanced, coasting along the shores of Calabria without losing sight of them; but at ten o'clock in the evening, just as they came abreast of the Gulf of Santa-Eufemia, Captain Courrand cut the rope which moored his boat to the vessel, and rowed away from the fleet.

Murat had thrown himself on to his bed without undressing; they brought him the news.

He rushed up to the deck, and arrived in time to see the boat, which was fleeing in the direction of Corsica, grow small and vanish in the distance. He remained motionless, not uttering a cry, giving no signs of rage; he only sighed and let his head fall on his breast: it was one more leaf falling from the exhausted tree of his hopes.

General Franceschetti profited by this hour of discouragement to advise him not to land in Calabria, and to go direct to Trieste, in order to claim from Austria the refuge which had been offered.

The king was going through one of those periods of extreme exhaustion, of mortal depression, when courage quite gives way: he refused flatly at first, and there at last agreed to do it.

Just then the general perceived a sailor lying on some coils of ropes, within hearing of all they said; he interrupted himself, and pointed him out to Murat.

The latter got up, went to see the man, and recognised Luidgi; overcome with exhaustion, he had fallen asleep on deck. The king satisfied himself that the sleep was genuine, and besides he had full confidence in the man. The conversation, which had been interrupted for a moment, was renewed: it was agreed that without saying anything about the new plans, they would clear Cape Spartivento and enter the Adriatic; then the king and the general went below again to the lower deck.

The next day, the 8th October, they found themselves abreast of Pizzo, when Joachim, questioned by Barbara as to what he proposed to do, gave the order to steer for Messina. Barbara answered that he was ready to obey, but that they were in need of food and water; consequently he offered to go on, board Cicconi's vessel and to land with him to get stores. The king agreed; Barbara asked for the passports which he had received from the allied powers, in order, he said, not to be molested by the local authorities.

These documents were too important for Murat to consent to part with them; perhaps the king was beginning to suspect: he refused. Barbara insisted; Murat ordered him to land without the papers; Barbara flatly refused.

The king, accustomed to being obeyed, raised his riding-whip to strike the Maltese, but, changing his resolution, he ordered the soldiers to prepare their arms, the officers to put on full uniform; he himself set the example. The disembarkation was decided upon, and Pizzo was to become the Golfe Juan of the new Napoleon.

Consequently the vessels were steered for land. The king got down into a boat with twenty-eight soldiers and three servants, amongst whom was Luidgi. As they drew near the shore General Franceschetti made a movement as if to land, but Murat stopped him.

"It is for me to land first," he said, and he sprang on shore.

He was dressed in a general's coat, white breeches and riding-boots, a belt carrying two pistols, a gold-embroidered hat with a cockade fastened in with a clasp made of fourteen brilliants, and lastly he carried under his arm the banner round which he hoped to rally his partisans. The town clock of Pizzo struck ten. Murat went straight up to the town, from which he was hardly a hundred yards distant. He followed the wide stone staircase which led up to it.

It was Sunday. Mass was about to be celebrated, and the whole population had assembled in the Great Square when he arrived. No one recognised him, and everyone gazed with astonishment at the fine officer. Presently he saw amongst the peasants a former sergeant of his who had served in his guard at Naples. He walked straight up to him and put his hand on the man's shoulder.

"Tavella," he said, "don't you recognise me?"

But as the man made no answer:

"I am Joachim Murat, I am your king," he said. "Yours be the honour to shout 'Long live Joachim!' first."

Murat's suite instantly made the air ring with acclamations, but the Calabrians remained silent, and not one of his comrades took up the cry for which the king himself had given the signal; on the contrary, a low murmur ran through the crowd. Murat well understood this forerunner of the storm.

"Well," he said to Tavella, "if you won't cry 'Long live Joachim!' you can at least fetch me a horse, and from sergeant I will promote you to be captain."

Tavella walked away without answering, but instead of carrying out the king's behest, went into his house, and did not appear again.

In the meantime the people were massing together without evincing any of the sympathy that the king had hoped for. He felt that he was lost if he did not act instantly.

"To Monteleone!" he cried, springing forward towards the road which led to that town.

"To Monteleone!" shouted his officers and men, as they followed him.

And the crowd, persistently silent, opened to let them pass.

But they had hardly left the square before a great disturbance broke out. A man named Giorgio Pellegrino came out of his house with a gun and crossed the square, shouting, "To your arms!"

He knew that Captain Trenta Capelli commanding the Cosenza garrison was just then in Pizzo, and he was going to warn him.

The cry "To arms!" had more effect on the crowd than the cry "Long live Joachim!"

Every Calabrian possesses a gun, and each one ran to fetch his, and when Trenta Capelli and Giorgio Pellegrino came back to the square they found nearly two hundred armed men there.

They placed themselves at the head of the column, and hastened forward in pursuit of the king; they came up with him about ten minutes from the square, where the bridge is nowadays. Seeing them, Murat stopped and waited for them.

Trenta Capelli advanced, sword in hand, towards the king.

"Sir," said the latter, "will you exchange your captain's epaulettes for a general's? Cry 'Long live Joachim!' and follow me with these brave fellows to Monteleone."

"Sire," said Trenta Capelli, "we are the faithful subjects of King Ferdinand, and we come to fight you, and not to bear you company. Give yourself up, if you would prevent bloodshed."

Murat looked at the captain with an expression which it would be impossible to describe; then without deigning to answer, he signed to Cagelli to move away, while his other hand went to his pistol. Giotgio Pellegrino perceived the movement.

"Down, captain, down!" he cried. The captain obeyed. Immediately a bullet whistled over his head and brushed Murat's head.

"Fire!" commanded Franceschetti.

"Down with your arms!" cried Murat.

Waving his handkerchief in his right hand, he made a step towards the peasants, but at the same moment a number of shots were fired, an officer and two or three men fell. In a case like this, when blood has begun to flow, there is no stopping it.

Murat knew this fatal truth, and his course of action was rapidly decided on. Before him he had five hundred armed men, and behind him a precipice thirty feet high: he sprang from the jagged rock on which he was standing, and alighting on the sand, jumped up safe and sound. General Franceschetti and his aide-de-camp Campana were able to accomplish the jump in the same way, and all three went rapidly down to the sea through the little wood which lay within a hundred yards of the shore, and which hid them for a few moments from their enemies.

As they came out of the wood a fresh discharge greeted them, bullets whistled round them, but no one was hit, and the three fugitives went on down to the beach.

It was only then that the king perceived that the boat which had brought them to land had gone off again. The three ships which composed the fleet, far from remaining to guard his landing, were sailing away at full speed into the open sea.

The Maltese, Barbara, was going off not only with Murat's fortune, but with his hopes likewise, his salvation, his very life. They could not believe in such treachery, and the king took it for some manoeuvre of seamanship, and seeing a fishing-boat drawn up on the beach on some nets, he called to his two companions, "Launch that boat!"

They all began to push it down to the sea with the energy of despair, the strength of agony.

No one had dared to leap from the rock in pursuit of them; their enemies, forced to make a detour, left them a few moments of liberty.

But soon shouts were heard: Giorgio Pellegrino, Trenta Capelli, followed by the whole population of Pizzo, rushed out about a hundred and fifty paces from where Murat, Franceschetti, and Campana were straining themselves to make the boat glide down the sand.

These cries were immediately followed by a volley. Campana fell, with a bullet through his heart.

The boat, however, was launched. Franceschetti sprang into it, Murat was about to follow, but he had not observed that the spurs of his riding-boots had caught in the meshes of the net. The boat, yielding to the push he gave it, glided away, and the king fell head foremost, with his feet on land and his face in the water. Before he had time to pick himself up, the populace had fallen on him: in one instant they had torn away his epaulettes, his banner, and his coat, and would have torn him to bits himself, had not Giorgio Pellegrino and Trenta Capelli taken him under their protection, and giving him an arm on each side, defended him in their turn against the people. Thus he crossed the square as a prisoner where an hour before he had walked as a king.

His captors took him to the castle: he was pushed into

the common prison, the door was shut upon him, and the king found himself among thieves and murderers, who, not knowing him, took him for a companion in crime, and greeted him with foul language and hoots of derision.

A quarter of an hour later the door of the gaol opened and Commander Mattei came in: he found Murat standing with head proudly erect and folded arms. There was an expression of indefinable loftiness in this half-naked man whose face was stained with blood and bespattered with mud. Mattei bowed before him.

"Commander," said Murat, recognising his rank by his epaulettes, "look round you and tell me whether this is a prison for a king."

Then a strange thing happened: the criminals, who, believing Murat their accomplice, had welcomed him with vociferations and laughter, now bent before his royal majesty, which had not overawed Pellegrino and Trenta Capelli, and retired silently to the depths of their dungeon.

Misfortune had invested Murat with a new power.

Commander Mattei murmured some excuse, and invited Murat to follow him to a room that he had had prepared for him; but before going out, Murat put his hand in his pocket and pulled out a handful of gold and let it fall in a shower in the midst of the gaol.

"See," he said, turning towards the prisoners, "it shall not be said that you have received a visit from a king, prisoner and crownless as he is, without having received largesse."

"Long live Joachim!" cried the prisoners.

Murat smiled bitterly. Those same words repeated by the same number of voices an hour before in the public square, instead of resounding in the prison, would have made him King of Naples.

The most important events proceed sometimes from such mere trifles, that it seems as if God and the devil must throw dice for the life or death of men, for the rise or fall of empires.

Murat followed Commander Mattei: he led him to a little room which the porter had put at his disposal. Mattei was going to retire when Murat called him back.

"Commander," he said, "I want a scented bath."

"Sire, it will be difficult to obtain."

"Here are fifty ducats; let someone buy all the eau de Cologne that can be obtained. Ah—and let some tailors be sent to me."

"It will be impossible to find anyone here capable of making anything but a peasant's clothes."

"Send someone to Monteleone to fetch them from there."

The commander bowed and went out.

Murat was in his bath when the Lavaliere Alcala was announced, a General and Governor of the town. He had sent damask coverlets, curtains, and arm-chairs. Murat was touched by this attention, and it gave him fresh composure. At two o'clock the same day General Nunziante arrived from Santa-Tropea with three thousand men. Murat greeted his old acquaintance with pleasure; but at the first word the king perceived that he was before his judge, and that he had not come for the purpose of making a visit, but to make an official inquiry.

Murat contented himself with stating that he had been on his way from Corsica to Trieste with a passport from the Emperor of Austria when stormy weather and lack of provisions had forced him to put into Pizzo. All other questions Murat met with a stubborn silence; then at least, wearied by his importunity—

"General," he said, "can you lend me some clothes after my bath?"

The general understood that he could expect no more information, and, bowing to the king, he went out. Ten minutes later, a complete uniform was brought to Murat; he put it on immediately, asked for a pen and ink, wrote to the commander-in-chief of the Austrian troops at Naples, to the English ambassador, and to his wife, to tell them of his detention at Pizzo. These letters written, he got up and paced his room for some time in evident agitation; at last, needing fresh air, he opened the window. There was a view of the very beach where he had been captured.

Two men were digging a hole in the sand at the foot of the little redoubt. Murat watched them mechanically. When the two men had finished, they went into a neighbouring house and soon came out, bearing a corpse in their arms.

The king searched his memory, and indeed it seemed to him that in the midst of that terrible scene he had seen someone fall, but who it was he no longer remembered. The corpse was quite without covering, but by the long black hair and youthful outlines the king recognised Campana, the aide-decamp he had always loved best.

This scene, watched from a prison window in the twilight, this solitary burial on the shore, in the sand, moved Murat more deeply than his own fate. Great tears filled his eyes and fell silently down the leonine face. At that moment General Nunziante came in and surprised him with outstretched arms and face bathed with tears. Murat heard him enter and turned round, and seeing the old soldier's surprise.

"Yes, general," he said, "I weep; I weep for that boy, just twenty-four, entrusted to me by his parents, whose death I have brought about. I weep for that vast, brilliant future which is buried in an unknown grave, in an enemy's country, on a hostile shore. Oh, Campana! Campana! if ever I am king again, I will raise you a royal tomb."

The general had had dinner served in an adjacent room. Murat followed him and sat down to table, but he could not eat. The sight which he had just witnessed had made him heartbroken, and yet without a line on his brow that man had been through the battles of Aboukir, Eylau, and Moscow! After dinner, Murat went into his room again, gave his various letters to General Nunziante, and begged to be left alone. The general went away.

Murat paced round his room several times, walking with long steps, and pausing from time to time before the window, but without opening it.

At last he overcame a deep reluctance, put his hand on the bolt and drew the lattice towards him.

It was a calm, clear night: one could see the whole shore. He looked for Campana's grave. Two dogs scratching the sand showed him the spot.

The king shut the window violently, and without undressing threw himself onto his bed. At last, fearing that his agitation would be attributed to personal alarm, he undressed and went to bed, to sleep, or seem to sleep all night.

On the morning of the 9th the tailors whom Murat had asked for arrived. He ordered a great many clothes, taking the trouble to explain all the details suggested by his fastidious taste. He was thus employed when General Nunziante came in. He listened sadly to the king's commands. He had just received telegraphic despatches ordering him to try the King of Naples by court-martial as a public enemy. But he found the king so confident, so tranquil, almost cheerful indeed, that he had not the heart to announce his trial to him, and took upon himself to delay the opening of operation until he received written instructions. These arrived on the evening of the 12th. They were couched in the following terms:

NAPLES, October 9, 1815

"Ferdinand, by the grace of God, etc . . . . wills and decrees the following:

"Art. 1. General Murat is to be tried by court-martial, the members whereof are to be nominated by our Minister of War.

"Art. 2. Only half an hour is to be accorded to the condemned for the exercises of religion.

"(Signed) FERDINAND."

Another despatch from the minister contained the names of the members of the commission. They were:—

Giuseppe Fosculo, adjutant, commander-in-chief of the staff, president.

Laffaello Scalfaro, chief of the legion of Lower Calabria.

Latereo Natali, lieutenant-colonel of the Royal Marines.

Gennaro Lanzetta, lieutenant-colonel of the Engineers.

W. T. captain of Artillery.

Francois de Venge, ditto.

Francesco Martellari, lieutenant of Artillery.

Francesco Froio, lieutenant in the 3rd regiment of the line.

Giovanni delta Camera, Public Prosecutor to the Criminal Courts of Lower Calabria.

Francesco Papavassi, registrar.

The commission assembled that night.

On the 13th October, at six o'clock in the morning, Captain Stratti came into the king's prison; he was sound asleep. Stratti was going away again, when he stumbled against a chair; the noise awoke Murat.

"What do you want with me, captain?" asked the king.

Stratti tried to speak, but his voice failed him.

"Ah ha!" said Murat, "you must have had news from

Naples."

"Yes, sire," muttered Stratti.

"What are they?" said Murat.

"Your trial, sire."

"And by whose order will sentence be pronounced, if you please? Where will they find peers to judge me? If they consider me as a king, I must have a tribunal of kings; if I am a marshal of France, I must have a court of marshals; if I am a general, and that is the least I can be, I must have a jury of generals."

"Sire, you are declared a public enemy, and as such you are liable to be judged by court-martial: that is the law which you instituted yourself for rebels."

"That law was made for brigands, and not for crowned heads, sir," said Murat scornfully. "I am ready; let them butcher me if they like. I did not think King Ferdinand capable of such an action."

"Sire, will you not hear the names of your judges?"

"Yes, sir, I will. It must be a curious list. Read it: I am listening."

Captain Stratti read out the names that we have enumerated. Murat listened with a disdainful smile.

"Ah," he said, as the captain finished, "it seems that every precaution has been taken."

"How, sire?"

"Yes. Don't you know that all these men, with the exception of Francesco Froio, the reporter; owe their promotion to me? They will be afraid of being accused of sparing me out of gratitude, and save one voice, perhaps, the sentence will be unanimous."

"Sire, suppose you were to appear before the court, to plead your own cause?"

"Silence, sir, silence!" said Murat. "I could, not officially recognise the judges you have named without tearing too many pages of history. Such tribunal is quite incompetent; I should be disgraced if I appeared before it. I know I could not save my life, let me at least preserve my royal dignity."

At this moment Lieutenant Francesco Froio came in to interrogate the prisoner, asking his name, his age, and his nationality. Hearing these questions, Murat rose with an expression of sublime dignity.

"I am Joachim Napoleon, King of the Two Sicilies," he answered, "and I order you to leave me."

The registrar obeyed.

Then Murat partially dressed himself, and asked Stratti if he could write a farewell to his wife and children. The Captain no longer able to speak, answered by an affirmative sign; then Joachim sat down to the table and wrote this letter:

"DEAR CAROLINE OF MY HEART,—The fatal moment has come: I am to suffer the death penalty. In an hour you will be a widow, our children will be fatherless: remember me; never forget my memory. I die innocent; my life is taken from me unjustly.

"Good-bye, Achilles good-bye, Laetitia; goodbye, Lucien; good-bye, Louise.

"Show yourselves worthy of me; I leave you in a world and

in a kingdom full of my enemies. Show yourselves superior to adversity, and remember never to think yourselves better than you are, remembering what you have been.

"Farewell. I bless you all. Never curse my memory. Remember that the worst pang of my agony is in dying far from my children, far from my wife, without a friend to close my eyes. Farewell, my own Caroline. Farewell, my children. I send you my blessing, my most tender tears, my last kisses. Farewell, farewell. Never forget your unhappy father,

"Pizzo, Oct. 13, 1815"

[We can guarantee the authenticity of this letter, having copied it ourselves at Pizzo, from the Lavaliere Alcala's copy of the original]

Then he cut off a lock of his hair and put it in his letter. Just then General Nunziante came in; Murat went to him and held out his hand.

"General," he said, "you are a father, you are a husband, one day you will know what it is to part from your wife and sons. Swear to me that this letter shall be delivered."

"On my epaulettes," said the general, wiping his eyes. [Madame Murat never received this letter.]

"Come, come, courage, general," said Murat; "we are soldiers, we know how to face death. One favour—you will let me give the order to fire, will you not?"

The general signed acquiescence: just then the registrar came in with the king's sentence in his hand.

Murat guessed what it was.

"Read, sir," he said coldly; "I am listening."

The registrar obeyed. Murat was right.

The sentence of death had been carried with only one dissentient voice.

When the reading was finished, the king turned again to Nunziante.

"General," he said, "believe that I distinguish in my mind the instrument which strikes me and the hand that wields that instrument. I should never have thought that Ferdinand would have had me shot like a dog; he does not hesitate apparently before such infamy. Very well. We will say no more about it. I have challenged my judges, but not my executioners. What time have you fixed for my execution?"

"Will you fix it yourself, sir?" said the general.

Murat pulled out a watch on which there was a portrait of his wife; by chance he turned up the portrait, and not the face of the watch; he gazed at it tenderly.

"See, general," he said, showing it to Nunziante; "it is a portrait of the queen. You know her; is it not like her?"

The general turned away his head. Murat sighed and put away the watch.

"Well, sire," said the registrar, "what time have you fixed?"

"Ah yes," said Murat, smiling, "I forgot why I took out my watch when I saw Caroline's portrait."

Then he looked at his watch again, but this time at its face.

"Well, it shall be at four o'clock, if you like; it is past three o'clock. I ask for fifty minutes. Is that too much, sir?"

The registrar bowed and went out. The general was about

to follow him.

"Shall I never see you again, Nunziante?" said Murat.

"My orders are to be present at your death, sire, but I cannot do it."

"Very well, general. I will dispense with your presence at the last moment, but I should like to say farewell once more and to embrace you."

"I will be near, sire."

"Thank you. Now leave me alone."

"Sire, there are two priests here."

Murat made an impatient movement.

"Will you receive them?" continued the general.

"Yes; bring them in."

The general went out. A moment later, two priests appeared in the doorway. One of them was called Francesco Pellegrino, uncle of the man who had caused the king's death; the other was Don Antonio Masdea.

"What do you want here?" asked Murat.

"We come to ask you if you are dying a Christian?"

"I am dying as a soldier. Leave me."

Don Francesco Pellegrino retired. No doubt he felt ill at ease before Joachim. But Antonio Masdea remained at the door.

"Did you not hear me?" asked the king.

"Yes, indeed," answered the old man; "but permit me, sire, to hope that it was not your last word to me. It is not the first time that I see you or beg something of you. I have already had occasion to ask a favour of you."

"What was that?"

"When your Majesty came to Pizzo in 1810, I asked you for 25,000 francs to enable us to finish our church. Your Majesty sent me 40,000 francs."

"I must have foreseen that I should be buried there," said Murat, smiling.

"Ah, sire, I should like to think that you did not refuse my second boon any more than my first. Sire, I entreat you on my knees."

The old man fell at Murat's feet.

"Die as a Christian!"

"That would give you pleasure, then, would it?" said the king.

"Sire, I would give the few short days remaining to me if God would grant that His Holy Spirit should fall upon you in your last hour."

"Well," said Murat, "hear my confession. I accuse myself of having been disobedient to my parents as a child. Since I reached manhood I have done nothing to reproach myself with."

"Sire, will you give me an attestation that you die in the Christian faith?"

"Certainly," said Murat.

And he took a pen and wrote: "I, Joachim Murat, die a Christian, believing in the Holy Catholic Church, Apostolic and Roman."

He signed it.

"Now, father," continued the king, "if you have a third

favour to ask of me, make haste, for in half an hour it will be too late."

Indeed, the castle clock was striking half-past three. The priest signed that he had finished.

"Then leave me alone," said Murat; and the old man went out.

Murat paced his room for a few moments, then he sat down on his bed and let his head fall into his hands. Doubtless, during the quarter of an hour he remained thus absorbed in his thoughts, he saw his whole life pass before him, from the inn where he had started to the palace he had reached; no doubt his adventurous career unrolled itself before him like some golden dream, some brilliant fiction, some tale from the Arabian Nights.

His life gleamed athwart the storm like a rainbow, and like a rainbow's, its two extremities were lost in clouds—the clouds of birth and death. At last he roused himself from this inward contemplation, and lifted a pale but tranquil face. Then he went to the glass and arranged his hair. His strange characteristics never left him. The affianced of Death, he was adorning himself to meet his bride.

Four o'clock struck.

Murat went to the door himself and opened it.

General Nunziante was waiting for him.

"Thank you, general," said Murat. "You have kept your word. Kiss me, and go at once, if you like."

The general threw himself into the king's arms, weeping, and utterly unable to speak.

"Courage," said Murat. "You see I am calm." It was this very calmness which broke the general's heart. He dashed out of the corridor, and left the castle, running like a madman.

Then the king walked out into the courtyard.

Everything was ready for the execution.

Nine men and a corporal were ranged before the door of the council chamber. Opposite them was a wall twelve feet high. Three feet away from the wall was a stone block: Murat mounted it, thus raising himself about a foot above the soldiers who were to execute him. Then he took out his watch,[Madame Murat recovered this watch at the price of 200 Louis] kissed his wife's portrait, and fixing his eyes on it, gave the order to fire. At the word of command five out of the nine men fired: Murat remained standing. The soldiers had been ashamed to fire on their king, and had aimed over his head. That moment perhaps displayed most gloriously the lionlike courage which was Murat's special attribute. His face never changed, he did not move a muscle; only gazing at the soldiers with an expression of mingled bitterness and gratitude, he said:

"Thank you; my friends. Since sooner or later you will be obliged to aim true, do not prolong my death-agonies. All I ask you is to aim at the heart and spare the face. Now——"

With the same voice, the same calm, the same expression, he repeated the fatal words one after another, without lagging, without hastening, as if he were giving an accustomed command; but this time, happier than the first, at the word "Fire!" he fell pierced by eight bullets, without a sigh, without a movement, still holding the watch in his left hand.

The soldiers took up the body and laid it on the bed where ten minutes before he had been sitting, and the captain put a guard at the door.

In the evening a man presented himself, asking to go into the death-chamber: the sentinel refused to let him in, and he demanded an interview with the governor of the prison. Led before him, he produced an order. The commander read it with surprise and disgust, but after reading it he led the man to the door where he had been refused entrance.

"Pass the Signor Luidgi," he said to the sentinel.

Ten minutes had hardly elapsed before he came out again, holding a bloodstained handkerchief containing something to which the sentinel could not give a name.

An hour later, the carpenter brought the coffin which was to contain the king's remains. The workman entered the room, but instantly called the sentinel in a voice of indescribable terror.

The sentinel half opened the door to see what had caused the man's panic.

The carpenter pointed to a headless corpse!

At the death of King Ferdinand, that, head, preserved in spirits of wine, was found in a secret cupboard in his bedroom.

A week after the execution of Pizzo everyone had received his reward: Trenta Capelli was made a colonel, General Nunziante a marquis, and Luidgi died from the effects of poison.

www.ingramcontent.com/pod-product-compliance
Lightning Source LLC
LaVergne TN
LVHW041309080426
835510LV00009B/928